WATERCOLOR
Methods for Students

CHRIS PETRI

ChrisPetri.com

For Students of All Levels

D1193326

ACKNOWLDGEMENTS

This book is dedicated to my parents Dolores and George, for their lifelong love, support and backing of my art career from its inception.

Many thanks to Lianne Procanyn, who designed and edited this book. I couldn't have completed this project without her expertise and efforts.

I owe a huge debt of gratitude to the many people throughout my life who have always help me to progress onwards and upwards. I also thank my many students from the United States and around the world. This book is for you!

PHOTOGRAPHY BY CHRIS PETRI

CONTENTS

INTRODUCTION

In this book I have crafted a basic and structured format for learning how to draw and paint in watercolor. I feel this book has a rythym that makes it comfortable to follow along with. I have added throughout this book details concerning technique and strategy for those who want new ideas and approaches to the watercolor medium, as well.

Whether you're just beginning your watercolor journey, or find yourself a seasoned and grizzled watercolor artist, there is much to learn and enjoy within these pages.

© Chris Petri 2022. All Rights Reserved.

Published by Kindle Direct Publishing.

All Paintings and photography by Chris Petri. All rights reserved. No part of this book may be reproduced or transmitted in any form of by any means, electronic, mechanical, photocopying, recording, or otherwise, without prior written permission of the publisher. For information, contact Amazon Kindle Publishing. Reviewers may quote brief passages in reviews.

PENCILS, BRUSHES, PAPER & OTHER STUFF

WATERCOLOR BRUSHES
AS PICTURED AND MY MOST FREQUENTLY-USED BRUSHES

- Da Vinci Maestro Tobolsky Kolinsky Sable 10 Germany #12, #14, #16 - Round Brushes
- Raphael - Matre Kolinsky Sable France 8404 - #6, #8 - Round Brushes
- Alvaro Castagnet Neef 4400 - #6, #8, Needle Point Brushes
- Escoda Reserva - Charles Reid - Sable Travel Brushes #6, #8, #10 - Set of 3 - Round Brushes
- Da Vinci Pure Kolinsky Sable - 1503 Germany - Travel Brush - #8, #10 - Round Brushes

PENCILS, PENS & MARKERS
AS PICTURED

- Alvin Draft/Matic Mechanical Pencil 0.5mm, 0.7mm and 0.9mm
- Pentel 120 A3 Mechanical Pencil 0.7mm and 0.9mm
- #2 Yellow Office Pencil

NOT PICTURED
- Staedtler Mars Lumograph Pencils
- Dixon Phano China Marker 77 black
- Sharpie Markers, Ultra fine point black and grey
- Uni Ball Vision Elite Black fine point pens

OTHER SUPPLIES

- Holbein Translucent Collapsible Water Containers, small size
- Holbein Mini Spritzer Bottle
- Small Kitchen Sponges
- Paper Towels
- Travel Tissues
- Scotch Drafting Tape #230, or Frog tape - yellow, green, or purple
- Fiskars Scissors
- Helix Ruler
- Titanium White Paint (for Touch Ups)
- Non-Slip Rug Pad
- Large Binder Clips

WATERCOLOR PAPER

- Fabriano Artistico Extra White Rough cold press 140lb/300gsm #10062-2042 full sheets
- Fabriano Studio Watercolor Pad 11"x14" cold press 140lb/300gsm
- Arches Rough cold press 140lb/300gsm gummed blocks
- Arches Satin Finish hot press 140lb/300gsm gummed blocks
- Canson hardbound spiral watercolor sketchbooks

- 2 -

DRAWING LAYOUT, PRELIMINARY SKETCHING AND CONTOUR DRAWING

DRAWING LAYOUT

As a watercolor artist, layout of your painting is highly important. Layout helps you to carefully transpose your subject matter onto the paper and within the rectangle of your sketchbook or sheet of paper. Whether you're working outdoors from photographs, electronic devices — such as a phone or TV screen — please carefully mark the outer borders of your paper at key points as shown in diagram 1. Please note that rulers, tape measures and artist/masking tape can be highly effective with marking out your hash marks around the borders of the painting.

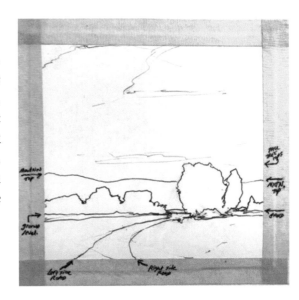

PRELIMINARY SKETCHING

When we start drawing our subject matter — whether it be still life, seascapes, landscapes, etcetera — it's important to render an extremely-light sketch of the the scene and subject matter. Remember to start with Layout and the hash marks at the borders of your drawing, as I did in Example 1. Here in Example 2, you can see I didn't add many details, however, I created a very light sillouette, of sorts. Once we complete the light Preliminary Sketch we can move onto the Contour Drawing.

CONTOUR DRAWING

Now as you're creating your Contour Drawing, it's more of a fun and relaxed time, as you use the light sketch underneath to keep you on course. It's best to start in a central location of the drawing, such as the flower bouquet. Slowly Contour Draw around the picture using the lines and shapes you have already drawn in. Don't worry about the light Sketch underneath; the painting process will cover practically all light sketch lines, as well as the Contour Drawing lines. If you enjoy the look of the pencil lines showing through, all the more you will not be worrying about lightening up on the pencil lines throughout the drawing process.

TONAL VALUES & MIXING COLORS

Accurate Tonal Values impact the look of your watercolor art in profound ways. As an Artist capturing a realistic look with spot-on "lights and darks" is worth a detailed study. Notice in the Tonal Value Chart (above), there are six tonal values turning light to dark, from left to right. The most straightforward way to create this chart on your own, is to use very little paint and more water for the light boxes and use almost no water and mostly all paint for the darker boxes on the right. Recall that all of the practice lessons and paintings in this book will require that you have soft, moist, and juicy watercolor paint in your palette or paint box. Using a dry watercolor palette will not work to achieve a successful watercolor painting with accurate tonal values. You will find frustration trying to scrub and activate dry paint in your palette while your watercolor washes are drying on your paper. You must be able to eventually work more rapidly and with a rythym in the watercolor medium. Accurate tonal values and a properly-prepared palette or paint box is one of the most important fundamentals for your watercolor art.

THE PINT / QUART / GALLON

The Pint / Quart / Gallon method is a word picture for the simple explanation of creating an extremely pleasant looking Tonal Value Patterns in a painting. Filmmakers and photographers use the Pint / Quart / Gallon method on a consistent basis. Let us do the same when creating our paintings. This has been a long and time-tested formula for great light and dark patterns. Below you will see three of my favorite Pint / Quart / Gallon Patterns. Try these Patterns out first by drawing a light preliminary sketch. Next, paint in an Ivory Black or Sepia watercolor paint to create the tonal value composition. I used Fabriano Artistico Extra White Rough.

PATTERN 1
A Pint of Darks, a Quart of Middle Tonal Values and a Gallon of Lights. I really enjoy this pattern, because I tend to leave quite a bit of white paper in my paintings. This scene reminds me of a hot and sunny Southwestern farm scene.

PATTERN 2
A Pint of Lights, a Quart of Darks and a Gallon of Middle Tonal Values. This is another fun patten and I would say this is what I use quite frequently along with Pattern 1. A great Landscape scene here, where we can feel the vast open space of a mountain and woods.

PATTERN 3
A Pint of Lights, a Quart of Middle Tonal Values and a Gallon of Darks. This I have used in quite a few Ink and Wash and Ink Paintings. Photographers who enjoy working in black and white would use this pattern quite frequently.

COLOR TONAL VALUE CHART

This is a great chart to create for yourself. In the Diagram below, you will notice the top row is the black and white chart we just reviewed and studied. Now, it is important to observe how the colors in our palette in their pure, undiluted state have a certain tonal value range. In other words, you will never create a very dark tonal value with yellow or orange hue or color, if you will. The same holds true that if you need an incredibly light tonal value, it will be difficult to create that with a blue or purple hue/color.

MIXING INTERESTING COLOR COMBINATIONS

My hope is that you will try creating color swatches of different and interesting combinations in your fun practice time. These swatches I did above were of exciting colors I really enjoy. Blue and Red is an incredibly-popular combination. Olive Green and Cad Orange, to me, is really exciting, enjoyable and relaxing. I recall a favorite polo shirt I used to wear for years and years: it was an olive green and cadmium orange, and had a large stripe pattern with white collar. A combination of Purple and Yellow is really fascinating. As an artist, try to jot down colors that seem to really catch your attention.

LOCAL COLOR - Red Delicious Apple
SMALL COMPOSITION/ STUDY

In this composition we will learn, importantly, what LOCAL COLOR is. Local Color is the inherent color of an object, independent of the effects of light and shadow upon it. Therefore, the center section of the apple is the "Local Color." The right side of the apple has light shining upon it. The left side of the apple is in shadow. One of the key takeaways here, is discerning what the Local Color of objects are from the start, and paint that first. Then we paint the shadows and light effects next.

1   Contour Draw the Apple. I used Fabriano Artistico Exrta White rough.

2   Paint in the bright red center of the apple with straight red tube paint.

3   Use a damp brush to blend a little bit of the red over to the right side of the apple.

4   Use more straight red paint with a touch of cobalt blue and ultramarine violet on the extreme left side of the apple.

- 3 -

PIGMENT AND PALETTES

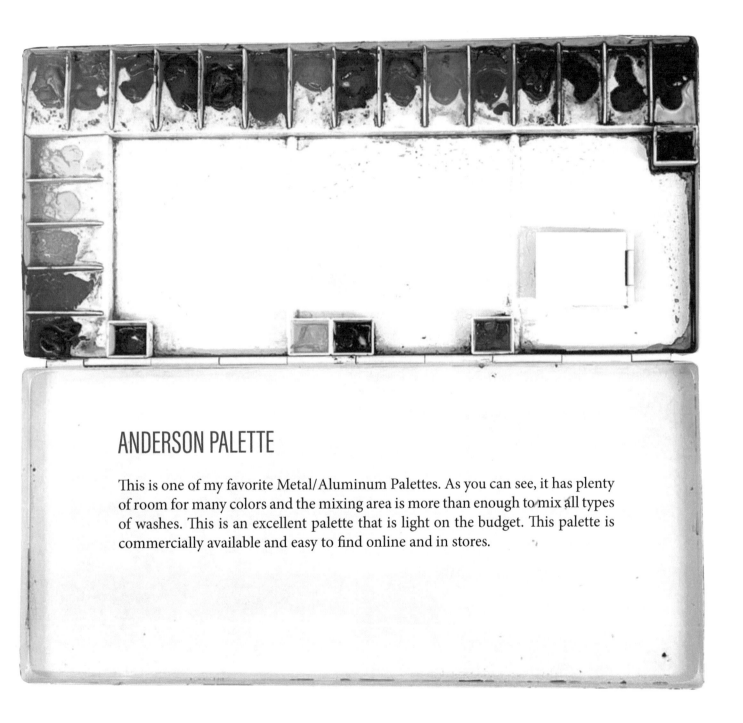

ANDERSON PALETTE

This is one of my favorite Metal/Aluminum Palettes. As you can see, it has plenty of room for many colors and the mixing area is more than enough to mix all types of washes. This is an excellent palette that is light on the budget. This palette is commercially available and easy to find online and in stores.

THE PALETTE BOX

This Palette is custom made by Craig Young in England. This is my favorite paint box I own and made of sturdy brass and coated with a great looking and highly-durable, white-baked enamel finish. This is great for small, to very large, paintings. This Palette is by custom order only.

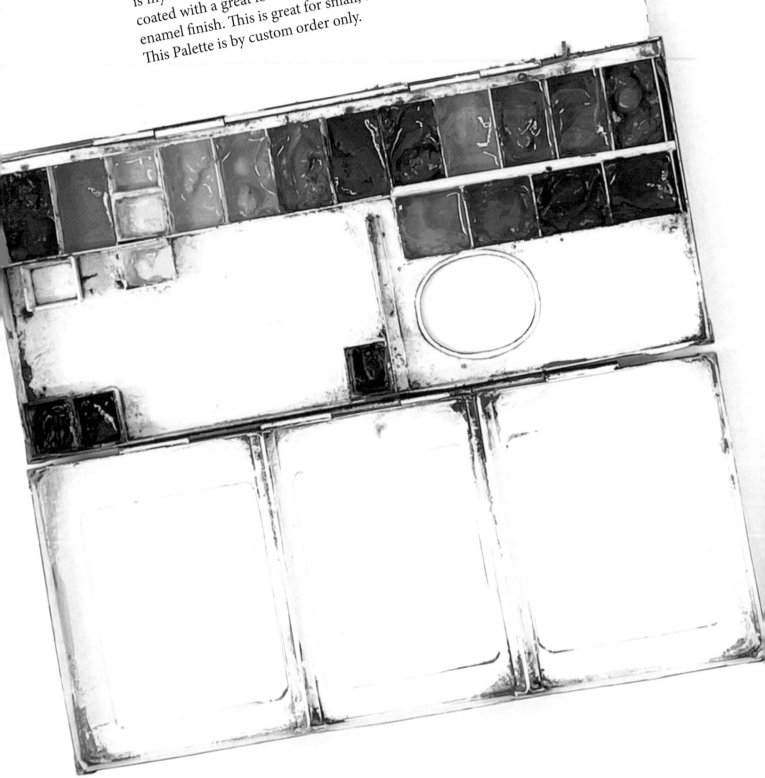

SCHMINCKE PALETTE - "MY YOUTUBE PALETTE"

This budget-friendly, light aluminum paint box/palette is my go-to palette for my YouTube videos. I installed my own half, and whole pans into the base with double stick tape. I was able to create more room for additional colors versus using the stock configuration. This palette is commercially available online and in stores.

USING FRESH, MOIST PAINT ALL OF THE TIME

One of the most important techniques used in this book it using wet and moist paint at all times when working on your watercolor art. Please note, that when you see vibrant, strong, intense colors in these paintings in this book, it is achieved by painting with a damp brush and fresh, moist paint. The way I keep my paints as if they are seemingly freshly squeezed out of the tube, is to place a small piece of damp paper towel in my palette at the end of the day and place it in a plastic bag. I then place it in a cool place, such as my mini fridge in my studio, or a cool window sill in winter. When I open it in the next session, it's ready to go with just a spritz of water. Even if I leave a particular paint box or palette unused for a few months in my mini fridge, the paints stay moist for that duration. I use most often Winsor & Newton and Holbein brands of watercolor paints.

– 4 –

BRUSHWORK

As an Artist, one of your most valuable skills is handling your watercolor brush with authority! If you practice these brush exercises and techniques regularly, I can say with confidence that the painting process, for you, will become seemingly effortless.

PARALLEL STROKE

Practice painting left to right and creating thin- to large-width brush strokes.

H STROKE

Follow the arrows on this diagram to create this swatch in any color of your liking.

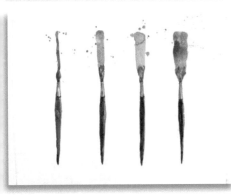

VERTICAL STROKE

Practice painting vertically top to bottom, varying the width of the brushstrokes.

S STROKE

Follow the arrows on the diagram to create this swatch in any color of your choosing.

SPLASHING AND SPATTERING

Practicing Splashing and Spattering on some scrap paper, so you get a feel for this technique.

Z STROKE

Follow the arrows on the diagram to create this swatch in any color you choose.

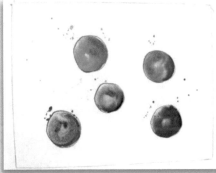

SPHERES

Draw circles and then Paint them in your favorite colors. Try to do these without lifting your brush off the paper by swirling the brush in circular motions.

LOST AND FOUND EDGES

When painting we want to accurately capture realistic tonal values, which we have said is extremely important. For Lost Edges, as the painting shows below, we will lose or merge our washes together when we find the tonal values are very close to equal. Notice that we keep the colors accurate to the subject matter when we merge the edges.

Now with Found Edges, we keep the identifiable light and dark contrast between two objects, or areas, in our painting. Please note that it is a very common that you will have continued occurrences of lost and found edges in your paintings. I have learned through study that if you can create approximately two thirds of your paining with lost edges and one third with found edges, this creates a very pleasant and pleasing look. It will not be possible to keep this ratio all of the time, however it's a good guide to keep in mind.

- 5 -

STILL LIFE

Pitcher and Orange

6" x 6" (15cm x 15cm)
STILL LIFE ON FABRIANO ARTISTICO EXTRA WHITE ROUGH COLD PRESS

MAIN TECHNIQUE: Ala Prima / Direct Approach

STUDIO PAINTING

MAIN COLORS: Olive Green, Sap Green, Raw Umber, Yellow Ochre, French Ultramarine Blue, Cadmium Orange, Cerulean Blue

1 Start painting the green leafy plants first, leaving fine stems and vine details for final touches to the painting after everything else is completed and dry.

2 The orange gets painted next, along with the shadows in the vase, light washes as you see.

3 Let everything dry 100% before adding in the very dark blue details on the vase. Those are done with straight paint and no water. Try leaving a large area of white paper with no washes on it at the left side of the vase and the left side of coffee cup. This is key to capturing the bright light you want in your painting.

Half Bottle of Wine

7" X 10" (18cm x 25cm)
STILL LIFE ON FABRIANO ARTISTICO
EXTRA WHITE ROUGH

MAIN TECHNIQUE: Ala Prima / Direct
Approach

SKETCHBOOK PAINTING

MAIN COLORS: Alizarin Crimson,
Cadmium Red, Burnt Sienna, Burnt Umber,
French Ultramarine Blue, Sap Green,
Viridian Green, Yellow Ochre, Raw Sienna,
Raw Umber, Prussian Blue, Ivory Black

The original was a sketchbook painting on somewhat-smooth Canson paper. If you have some off beat water spots, balloons, and blooms in your paintings, do not worry, they add variety to the overall look. Let things happen in your watercolor paintings, and always remember if you have a major problem, get a new sheet of paper and start anew.

1   I painted the wine bottle first, the glass of wine second, and finally, paintbrush.

2   I then take a quick twenty-minute break.

3   Now that all is dry, please have fun by adding in watery washes behind the glass-top table.

Ornate Tea Pot

7" X 9" (18cm x 23cm)
STILL LIFE ON FABRIANO ARTISTICO
EXTRA WHITE ROUGH

MAIN TECHNIQUE: Ala
Prima / Direct Approach

STUDIO PAINTING

MAIN COLORS: As many
blues as you like, Sap Green,
Ultramarine Violet, Alizarin
Crimson, Cadmium Red,
Cadmium Orange, Yellow
Ochre, Raw Sienna

1 Painting the medium and light shadows on the teapot first is a good idea, then taking a break to let that dry.

2 Now, paint the upper darks in the back drop second, once first wash is dry.

3 Add the final and beautiful flowery details on the teapot last with straight paint and no water added. These details should be painted on with the least amount of brush strokes as possible, almost a quick flick of the brush-type motion.

Recall to paint the darker background washes carefully up to the teapot, without using too much water in the washes. Keep in mind, watercolor washes dry about 40-50 percent lighter than the way they look when you put it on the paper, if you're adding an average amount of water to the wash mix! Note, that if you place straight-tube paint on your paper with no water mixed in it, it will dry with no fading or lightening.

Mug with Art Tools
STILL LIFE

This is a fun painting to create as we can draw and paint our familiar art tools!

1 Start out with a contour drawing, ensuring you are filling up your rectangle with subject matter.

2 We draw our mug first and then add in the pencils, pens brushes and other art tools we have.

3 Ensure the light is coming from the left side of the painting. Now you can paint in the shadow on the right side of the mug and art tools as you go.

4 Finishing up the painting, we add in the same repeating colors in the background areas behind the table and wall. Add in some splashes and spattering to create texture. Use a tissue to blot up some splashes if needed.

Green Wine Bottle
STILL LIFE

Creating a beautiful, green transparent wine bottle can transform your watercolor painting skills. Transparency is one of the unique qualities of watercolor, and use it to your advantage whenever you are able.

1   Start out with a preliminary sketch and then contour drawing. Make sure to fill up your rectangle with dominant subject matter.

2   Start your painting at the bottom of the bottle, working upwards. Have the bottle shadows at the base completed from the start, it needs to be fused together with the bottom of the bottle as you work upwards.

3   Recall that we are going to paint around the white label, as we are painting the green bottle colors. Let the wine bottle colors dry before adding the background colors. We can use all of our greens and reds for this painting, as well as yellow ochre and raw sienna, within the greens throughout. Recall, you want warm and cool everywhere in your paint mixtures, so greens are cool and golds are warm. Mix these both together as you create the hues of your wine bottle.

4   A few splashes here and there as you work on this painting will give it a more interesting and exciting look. However, overdoing any augmentation will cause an unpleasant feel to your paintings.

Beer, Lemon & Lime
STILL LIFE

We can create this lovely still life painting with confidence and control. Once we have the sketch completed, we can just enjoy the rich and vibrant colors of our palette.

1 We carefully create our preliminary sketch and go over top with our contour drawing.

2 We carefully start with the darks of burnt sienna, burnt umber, along with raw sienna. Also, add in the cools of cobalt blue, and cerulean blue.

3 After the beer bottle, we create the lime and lemon using our range of yellow and green colors.

4 Finally, we add in the background colors and stripes of the tablecloth. Remember to use almost no water while you paint 90% of this painting. The only time we will use a lot of water is in the light back drop washes behind the table. This wash gets painted in once everything else is completely dry, at the end of the painting.

Tulips Still Life

STILL LIFE

1. Creating this Flowers and Still Life should be fun and challenging at the same time. The difficult part is creating your layout, as we explained in detail in the beginning chapters.

2. Use a ruler to roughly layout the window dimensions and details, if free hand sketching doesn't seem to be working.

3. Next, we create a light Preliminary Sketch and move onto doing a Contour Drawing of the Flowers, Vase and objects on the table.

4. For painting, we create the vibrant and exciting colors of the tulips and fruit first, then finish up with the middle tonal values of the shadows and lighter washes in the painting. Remember to leave white on the paper on the window sill and table cloth.

Sunflower Still Life

5" X 7" (12cm x 17cm)
STILL LIFE ON FABRIANO
ARTISTICO EXTRA WHITE
ROUGH

STUDIO PAINTING
COLORS

1 I started first with my contour drawing, with two or three breaks as I went along.

2 Next, I started out painting in the center of the painting in the sunflower, vase, and pink flowers at the top.

3 The bottle, lemon, tomato and orange were painted next, making sure to paint the shadows underneath them right away, so they blend and mingle together.

4 Moving along and taking breaks, I finally paint in the shore bird and espresso cup.

5 Last task is to do the tablecloth stripes, background colors and a few splashes here and there, if you wish.

6 Notice that I did change a few things once I started painting. Do not worry if you make some minor changes once in a great while in your art as your working, if the painting says you need to.

– 6 –

FLOWERS

Fun Splashy Flowers in a Vase

SMALL COMPOSITION/ STUDY

1 Let's create a simple contour drawing and leave out the fine vinelike branches and twigs.

2 Start the painting with the dark greens and mixes of burnt sienna and blues in the top area of vase and then work on the upper leaves and splashy flower shapes.

3 Next, work on the lower vase area, making sure to leave white paper in the vase.

4 Lastly, paint the twigs, vines, and shadows in the vase area. Then do a few splashes up top, if you like, and put a touch of the same colors in the background wall beyond the table.

5 Paint this 10 times or until you have made it a masterpiece!

Foraged Pink Flowers

12" X 16" (30cm x 40cm)
FLOWERS - ARCHES SATIN FINISH ON
GUMMED BLOCK

STUDIO PAINTING

COLORS: All greens in my palette,
Cadmium Yellow Lemon, Ultramarine
Violet, Cerulean Blue, Cobalt Blue, Burnt
Sienna, Raw Sienna, Burnt Umber

1 After completing the preliminary and contour drawing, it's a good plan to start with darks. Let's begin with the dark greens just above the top of the vase.

2 Take breaks as you work, and I usually draw and paint left to right. So once I get that cluster of darks at the top of the vase, I start painting everything on the left part of the arrangement. I would paint in the twigs and stems close to last.

3 Background washes and splashes should be the last details. I also dabbed in some negative shape painting around the white flowers with cerulean blue, while the background wash was a tiny bit damp. Always enjoy creating your own fine details to your paintings!

Autumn Arrangement

9" X 12" (22cm x 30cm)

COLORS: I used all of the Red and Green Colors of my palette here, as well as Cadmium Yellow Lemon, Cobalt Blue and Ultramarine Violet.

STUDIO PAINTING

PAPER: Arches Satin Finish on gummed block

This painting does not have a corresponding contour drawing. Please feel free to have fun and and not have a strict game plan for your preliminary sketch and contour drawing.

1   Create Preliminary Sketch first to get the overall scale of things fairly accurate.

2   Create the Contour Drawing.

3   Begin painting the darks at the top of the vase, then to the left and work up the two sides of the arrangement lastly, and putting some light wash in the vase.

4   Finish up with the needle point brush, loosely painting in the twigs and branches as well, using a small round brush to paint in the berries.
They key to this painting is using the suggested brushes, especially the needle point brush. To create exciting details we must use the correct brushes to capture the essence of the subject matter.

Chris Peter
2022

– 7 –

LANDSCAPES & STREETSCAPES

Warm Up Landscape Compositions

Let's try a few small compositions to work out the feel for landscape scenes shall we?
Ok, lets go!

TOP LEFT – This is a sunlit field with interesting trees, bushes and distant purple mountains. The sky is loose and has a number of white clouds resting, as it seems, at the base of the sky and mountains. Painting these both Ala Prima or with the Glazing Technique works well. I often will go out into my backyard and just look at the trees, bushes, flowers, lawn and notice the light effects upon them. When you have leisure time, try to notice how the scenery changes with different weather patterns. For instance, shadows are longer in the early morning or late afternoon. At noon time, shadows are smaller and tend to fall directly under the subject matter. As an artist, take advantage of observing nature and the natural surroundings before you.

TOP RIGHT – This composition is really fun! There is much excitement in trying to recall a time you may have been on a dusty and rocky country road. Are you with me? Even a trip out to the countryside can get you in tune with your compositions and finished paintings. Fencing can create a great feeling of moving forward into the painting! I used very simple colors in the ground area, such as Burnt Umber, Raw Umber, Raw Sienna, Burnt Sienna, touch of Olive Green, Chromium of Oxide and Cerulean Blue. I mixed some Cobalt Blue and a tiny bit of the leftover colors in the palette to come up with the hazy sky. I used my needle point brush to create the interesting farm-like fence posts and barbed wires.

Grand Canal Venice Italy

7" X 6" (18CM X 15CM)
STREET SCENE ON ARCHES
ROUGH COLD PRESS

MAIN TECHNIQUE: Ala Prima / Direct Approach

STUDIO PAINTING

COLORS: Alizarin Crimson, Yellow Ochre, Cadmium Red, Cadmium Orange, French Ultramarine Blue, Cobalt Blue, Cerulean Blue, Prussian Blue, Viridian, Sap Green, Olive Green, Burnt Sienna, Burnt Umber, Ivory Black, Paynes Grey

My thoughts are that I have painted this style of architecture many times, so I can move quickly through the details. This painting is best completed in about two-to-three hours, with a few breaks here and there.

1   We start this painting with all of the darks first. So I added in the dark window and door areas, shutters, window trim and some dark shadows under the cornice.

2   Next, I add in the blues, greens, and golds of the window glass.

3   Next, I paint the water and sky washes and let that dry completely.

4   I wrap up by adding the salmon pink colored wash for the wall washes.

5   The finishing touches are the window and French door railings, along with the upper railing and clothesline pole.

The southern areas of the United States are absolutely beautiful and inspirational. I had the great fortune to live in North Carolina as a young boy in the mid-1970s. There were mountains, valleys, pine trees, winding roads, many sunny days and great people! I always think of the south as a relaxed style of living.

Let's unwind on a more laid-back painting, shall we? White structures always do much of the work for a watercolor artist. Painting shadows and textures upon them are tremendously exciting, I feel.

At the white stucco, I just splashed on some warm and cool splashes and spatters of Cadmium Orange, Alizarin Crimson, and Cerulean Blue. Starting the painting with all of the darks at the windows and then over to the roof, you will have an advantage this way.

Let the previous darks that were painted in dry 100 percent and then add in the lighter tonal values at lower windows and door. Next, add the shadows under the eaves of the roof with a middle tonal value. making sure to also get the angles correct. Your home-free now! Next, paint in the fields and bushes and, lastly, after all else is 100 percent dry, paint in the plants in the near foreground; that pushes the house back to make it feel more in the middle distance.

Southern Home

Sandy Hook Barracks

6″ X 8″ (15cm x 20cm)
Landscape on Fabriano
Artistico Extra White rough

MAIN TECHNIQUE: Ala
Prima/ Direct Approach

STUDIO PAINTING

COLORS: All the Colors of
my Palette

1 Please paint the dark washes of the roof first and then work into main building.

2 We then put in the washes of the distant hills and foreground.

3 Moving on, paint in the shadows of the building, details of the windows, and trees and then lastly, the sky washes.

Be careful not to paint with too much water in areas around the building. One of the keys to Ala Prima painting method, is to keep washes from re-activating other dry areas in the painting while working on new sections. Notice how the water behind the building gives the painting a good feel of depth?

Avalon Vacation – New Jersey Shore

7" X 10" (18cm x 25cm)
STREET SCENE ON CANSON HARDBOUND WATERCOLOR SKETCHBOOK
MAIN TECHNIQUE: Ala Prima / Direct Approach

SKETCHBOOK PAINTING PLEN AIR

COLORS: All the Colors of my Palette

I created the drawing and then started painting the shadow under the white railing first. Next, a break to get another cup of coffee.

1 Let's start painting the undulating rooftops while working into the trees and greenery. I feel a break is good at this point.

2 Finally, we loosely paint in the distant houses and streets, along with utility poles and lines.

3 This painting is a sketchbook painting I did while on vacation with my family quite a few summers ago. I was overlooking a gorgeous view of shore homes and a peaceful, early morning street.

Midwest Farm Scene

9" X 12" (22cm x 30cm)

LANDSCAPE ON ARCHES SATINE
GUMMED BLOCK

STUDIO PAINTING

Creating a relaxed farm scene is a pleasant experience. The mostly middle tonal values in this painting gives it a hazy day feel. With fields and barns as far as the eye can see, the viewer's eyes are drawn into the scene and allowed to meander around to the farthest-distant areas. I used all my greens I have in my palette, with Yellow Ochre, Alizarin Crimson and Burnt Sienna, for the warmest colors, and finally, all my blues and Ultramarine Violet for the coolest subject matter. This is a painting with strong depth of field.

As an Artist, one of your missions is to draw the viewer in and have them enjoy the scene for a while.

Farmhouse

Create your preliminary sketch and Contour Drawing, insuring that you have the correct overall layout of the design. Your roofs of the farmhouse should be approximately halfway on the paper, from top to bottom.

Take your time, gently penciling in the preliminary sketch and contour drawing,

Using Sepia Winsor & Newton paint, do the darkest darks first — the roofs, trees, horse and carriage at the road area, wind mill, and grass areas close to the farmhouse. Let these areas dry 100 percent.

Secondly, paint in the middle tonal values of the road, foreground fields and skies. Once they dry in approximately 15 to 20 minutes, you can add in the next washes.

Add the darks, such as the shadows under the fence posts, as well as any shadows under the farmhouse and trees that comprise the main subject matter of this painting. This should be the finished and polished look you're after!

City Seascape

Try different techniques and styles as you move forward in your watercolor journey. In this painting, we will use a glazing technique.

Start by applying a liberal and wet sky wash over the entire paper of Cobalt Blue, Cerulean Blue, with just a touch of raw umber here and there, for a warm and cool feel. Let this first wash dry 100 percent.

We now create a wash of Cerulean Bleu, French Ultramarine Blue, Burnt Sienna, Yellow Ochre, and Olive Green. Use these colors to create the skyline of the distant buildings and cityscape along the water. Take the same colors and flow them down into the water to create the reflections.

Create the reflections loosely and with a quick attitude versus fussing around to much. Watercolor is often better served up expeditiously.

Hazy Cityscape

We will use the watercolor medium to help create the lovely, hazy and misty cityscape views we are looking for. Always be willing to try different techniques and methods in the watercolor medium. We can use square or flat brushes for this painting, although it is not necessary. If you use round brushes, you will just have to be careful to paint the square edges of the buildings with better precision.

1 Create the light preliminary sketch and contour drawing first.

2 Next, create a wet wash of alizarin crimson and yellow ochre with a touch of cerulean blue across the entire painting area. Let this dry completely before starting your next washes.

3 Once the previous wash has completely dried, add in the medium tonal values of the buildings in the medium distance. These washes should be of warm and cool colors that are just a bit darker than the distant first sky wash you completed at the start.

4

Create the dark brick buildings with windows, and rooftop water tanks in the foreground of the painting, left and right sides last. Make sure to paint around the window rectangle shapes. We should use the darkest colors in our palette, French Ultramarine Blue, Burnt Umber, and Burnt Sienna, for the foreground buildings.

The Lamb Inn

This is a fun painting and easy for everyone to really have good success with! It has basic shapes, such as the triangle roofs, and many rectangles and squares for the windows and window panes. This is an Ala Prima painting, so we paint in the dark hues first.

1 We can start with a good rough sketch. We will do a large square and triangle on top for the main building.

2 Repeat the same, but smaller, for the left side of the main building.

3 We then add in the chimneys, as well as the figures, Lamb Inn wrought iron sign, and lastly, the car on the right.

4 Finally, we sketch in just a few very light lines for the cloud shapes.

5 We now start painting in the darks — just get all the warm and cool colors going! Fire them into the windows and door areas, as well as roof shingles, figures and car.

6 Finish up with the light tonal values of the painting in the sky and building stucco areas.

Coastal Lighthouse Rainshower

This is a fun painting with much atmosphere and emotion.

1 We create our preliminary sketch and Contour drawing first.

2 Next, we wet the sky area of the paper with fresh clean water from our water container.

3 Paint on your pre-moistened paper some cobalt blue and Paynes gray creating a dark rain cloud effect on the left side of the paining, letting the wash flow downwards. Let this wash dry 100 percent before moving on.

4 Next, we paint the lighthouse and sandy embankment it sits upon. We use our yellow ochre, sap green, olive green and cerulean blue to create the trees, sand and foliage.

5 Finish the last details of the distant ocean horizon line on the right side of the painting and we have a complete painting!

Loose Boats Lesson

We can get this painting completed quickly as we game plan carefully. The main focus is getting the preliminary and contour drawing done first. Then we start on the washes of beautiful vibrant paint.

1. We paint the viridian green and raw umber skyline first, letting that wash blend into the white paper underneath. Take a quick break and let the sky wash dry, approximately 10 to 15 minutes.

2. We paint the boats at the top section next with the ocean horizon line, being careful to leave white paper on the boats where the sunlight is striking them from the left. This is the key focal point of the painting; let's take our time and get things very accurate here.

3. Once you have the boats completed, paint in the rich and dark blue ocean horizon line. I used my darker blues and a touch of sap green and viridian.

4. As the darker ocean hues are painted in, let;s use cerulean and cobalt blue to create the lighter washes of the coastal waters at the right of the land area.

5. Once we have the water completed, take a 20 to 30 minute break and start on the light washes of the sandy hill in the foreground. I used green and gold hues lightly washed in here. Let this dry, too, before doing the rocks.

6. Create the rocks and loosely-painted tree last, using dark hues of browns and reds with touches dark blues, such as French Ultramarine Blue and Ultramarine Violet.

7. Finish with a hake and needle point brush for the foreground foilage and grasses, etc.

– 8 –

SEASCAPES

TOP COMP 1

I start with the dark ocean colors of blues and greens, with a touch of burnt sienna. Feel free to use tape above the waterline to keep the ocean looking level and neat with all of these comps. Work down towards the sand, getting lighter with less paint and lighter washes of viridian green and cerulean blue. Let the whole thing dry now completely. Finish by adding the yellow ochre and raw sienna beach and cobalt blue and French Ultramarine blue sky, adding just a very light amount of cadmium orange to the lower sky.

MIDDLE COMP 2

Start out same as COMP 1, except keep the distant ocean colors lighter in tonal value; let's say cobalt blue, with cerulean blue and a touch of your favorite green. I would use painter's tape on the ocean horizon line on this painting, too. Note: Keep some horizontal lines of white paper for the waves crashing into the shoreline. Also, making the sandy beach a bit on an angle is more interesting.

BOTTOM COMP 3

This was a cloudy and rainy day feel for this comp. Do you notice that the ocean horizon line is now at the lower third space division? We can use tape again for the waterline. Cobalt blue, French Ultramarine Blue and a touch of Viridian Green with Raw Sienna for the deep ocean area. Add Raw Sienna and Cerulean for the sandy foreground. Let dry completely and wash in the cloudy overcast sky and clouds. Let's use a touch of Paynes Gray, mixed with Raw Sienna and Cerulean Blue, for the cloudy and stormy feel of clouds and sky. Please notice that in the far distant sky just above the horizon line, I added some light horizontal cloud formations. This will bring an added feel of distance in the painting.

Quick Seascape Warm Up Study

In this quick composition you should frame out small- to medium-size rectangles with painters tape and create interesting seascape washes, as shown. Notice the space divisions of sky and ocean first, get that set and the rest is easy. Continue practicing until you get them looking the way you want them to. I used Fabriano Artistico Extra White paper for these studies.

Hemingway - Rockport, Maine

7" X 10" (18cm x 25cm)
SEASCAPES & BOATS ON CANSON
HARDBOUND WATERCOLOR SKETCHBOOK

MAIN TECHNIQUE: Ala Prima/
Direct Approach

SKETCHBOOK PAINTING PLEIN AIR

COLORS: All Blues And Greens, Cadmium
Lemon Yellow, Burnt Umber, Raw Umber,
Cadmium Red, Alizarin Crimson, Yellow
Ochre

1 Start the closest boat first, perhaps drawing it a few times on some sketch paper to get the feel of the angles and curves.

2 The distant boat would be second, tying it into the distant shoreline.

3 Finish up the hills and blue washes of the cool water to complete the painting.

4 I left a lot of white paper on this painting, as I was working at a faster tempo. This was a sketchbook painting done on location, not far from the Charles Reid Workshop I was attending a number of summers ago. I recall I was seated at a picnic table in a beautiful cove, the weather was slightly overcast. It was a comforting feeling being surrounded by a high, rocky embankment around the inlet.

Fishing Boats

14" X 10" (36cm x 25cm)
SEASCAPE: Fabriano
Artistico Extra White Rough
MAIN TECHNIQUE:
Ala Prima/ Direct Approach
COLORS - All Colors of my
Palette

PLEIN AIR

Drawing and Painting on a summer weekend excursion lead me to a quiet inlet with fishing boats and small shacks.

1 I carefully started the drawing and then painted the large boat on the left.

2 I painted in the green and blue water of the cove, once the large boat on left dried substantially,

3 Next, we put in the details of the middle distance, making those washes a bit more cooler in color temperature, as it gives a feeling of distance.

4 Once home in my studio, I added in the light washes of the sky and also used my needlepoint brush to create some fine detail of ropes, rigging and a small communications tower in the middle distance.

5 A quick note for Plein Air painting: If you think your subject matter my move or go away, get that part done first in your painting. After that, continue on with the rest of the drawing and painting on location or at the home studio.

Sunny Day at the Beach

Seascape on Canson Hardbound watercolor Sketchbook

MAIN TECHNIQUE: Ala Prima / Direct Approach

STUDIO PAINTING

COLORS: French Ultramarine Blue, Cobalt Blue, Cerulean Blue, Viridian Green, Yellow Ochre, Cadmium Orange, Alizarin Crimson, Burnt Umber, Cadmium Lemon Yellow, Ultramarine Violet, Titanium White

1   I tape down the ocean horizon line first with frog tape. The key is we paint under the tape, so the top of the ocean is the sharp dark line at the top once we pull up the tape. Use a ruler or tape measure with hash marks on the edges of the drawing to make sure the ocean line is level and not tipping downward in either direction.

2   Let's paint the hurricane fence in second, making sure the ocean water has dried 100 percent before doing so.

3   Create the sky washes last, making it a fun freestyle application of washes. You will notice I play down my sky washes on many occasions.

4   Once all is 100 percent dry, paint in the purple shadows of the fence. A great observation I made in watercolor early on was the importance of being very aware of what was wet, damp, and dry on my paper as I painted. This consideration will serve you well as you paint in the watercolor medium.

An interesting side note is I have created this scene many times in similar forms. I recall back in the late 1980's creating this scene on a white canvas board with the wet on wet oil painting method. These painting shows were shown on public TV often in the 80's and 90's. I think it is good to create drawings and painting from scratch or our imagination occasionally. It helps if you need to add or delete something into a painting or rearrange some subject matter. If you have practiced the improvisation process it will feel comfortable after a while. Hence you will have another tool in the toolbox.

Quick Boat Study

This is a quick study of a number of simple fishing boats in a quiet inlet.

1. I used the glazing technique in this painting, starting with an overall light- to medium-blue wash in the sky and water and then adding in a tiny bit of cadmium orange in the bottom of the sky.

2. Once completely dry, I added in the distant blue green hills and weeds and brush in foreground.

3. Finally, I added the boats, a few splashes, spattering and a lighter version of the hills in the left area of water.

Coastal Waters

As we paint this coastal scene, let us notice how beautiful the scene looks with the big sky and low-lying marshes. I used Arches satin paper on this painting.

1. Let's start out with a wet wash of Cobalt and French Ultramarine Blue, all the way from top to bottom of the paper.

2. Add just a bit of yellow ochre along the horizon line as we are finishing up the first washes. Now, let these washes dry 100 percent before you move onto the foreground.

3. Add in the medium distance and foreground washes of the muddy marshes with darker pigment, such as Raw Umber, Burnt Umber, Yellow Ochre and a touch of French Ultramarine Blue.

4. Use a tissue to blot up some water when you are creating the sky washes, if necessary.

Sunrise in Venice

A coffee-table book can inspire us to create wonderful paintings. This was an "into the light" painting. The sun is rising behind these beautiful buildings in Venice! Let us enjoy the architecture as we paint. Colors here were heavy on the darker and warmer side with a lot of Raw Sienna, Raw Umber and Yellow Ochre hues. The sky is bright so I did really light washes of mostly-light blues and earlier mixes I had for the buildings in the skyline.

Rockland Breakwater Lighthouse

5" X 8" (13cm x 20cm)

MAIN TECHNIQUE: Ala Prima/ Direct Approach

Sketchbook Painting Plen Air

SEASCAPES & BOATS on Canson Hardbound watercolor Sketchbook

COLORS: All Blues and Greens, Ultramarine Violet, Cadmium Lemon Yellow, Yellow Ochre, Burnt Umber, Raw Umber, Cadmium Red, Alizarin Crimson, Yellow Ochre, Ivory Black, Paynes Gray

1 I paint the upper structure of Lighthouse first

2 Next, we paint in the concrete and stone foundation.

3 The distant hills and trees go in third.

4 The bay water is next in the process, with the Sky washes last. The darkest darks of the Lighthouse are painted with pure pigment and a damp brush. The reds are painted the same, with just a tiny bit of water. The stone foundation, water, and distant hills are painted with a little more water and a fair amount of pigment. The distant darker trees and bushes are straight pigment into the damp green washes. If I painted this again, I would diminish some of the fine-lined details in the Lighthouse foundation. Improvements can always be made, either by adding or deleting subject matter, during all phases of the picture-making process. You will learn with every painting.

A Day at the Beach

6" X 8" (15cm x 20cm)
Portraits And Figures on Canson Hardbound
Watercolor Sketchbook

MAIN TECHNIQUE: Ala Prima/ Direct Approach

Sketchbook Painting Plein Air

COLORS: All Blues And Greens, Yellow Ochre,
Cadmium Red, Burnt Sienna, Burnt Umber,
Ultramarine Violet

1   Start painting the man in the lawn chair first and then the woman on the left.

2   The dark washes of the distant ocean is second on the agenda, with the middle distance ocean water third.

3   Lastly, we add in the light washes of the sky and beach area. Note that each step in the painting should be painted at a successively faster tempo.

4   The figures are painted carefully and slow, from then on forward ,you will pick up the pace each step of the way in the process. The last light washes of the sky and beach are painted quickly, in a fun and carefree fashion.

Always remember to paint some really fun and carefree paintings on office printer paper in your spare time. What you practice will show up in your finished paintings!

Avalon Beach, Sept 17th 2016 - 6"x8"

Boats in Harbour

This is a fun painting we will paint here! This is a Glazing Technique Style Painting. We first splash in the sky washes and blend it down into entire bottom section of the painting.

1   Start by adding some fresh, clean water to dampen the sky areas in a random way, leaving some dry areas of paper, too.

2   Work the cool sky color washes down into the water and shoreline areas. Once this is completed, let the whole watercolor paper area dry 100 percent.

3   Next, start painting all of the greens, yellows and umbers into the shore areas, creating the boat shapes, tree shapes, as well as the boat house on pilings on the left.

4   Use your needlepoint brush to create the final details of the boat masts and rigging lines once all the other areas of the painting have completely dried.

5   Recall, when painting in the reflections of the boats, masts, and pilings of the dock, keep those reflections wavy and leave them looking like a dashed-line pattern, versus a straight line. We want to break up, or interrupt if you will, those lines whenever possible.

6   Please note, that we should add just a very little amount of the colors in the bottom of the painting into the sky wash, but very little. This will pay big dividends in having your painting look harmonized throughout. It is extremely difficult to create a pleasant and pleasing painting with blocks of separate hues.

PORTRAITS

PORTRAIT PAINTING.

Western Cowboy

7" X 7" (18cm x 18cm)
Portrait & Figures on Fabiano Studio Watercolor Cold Press

MAIN TECHNIQUE: Ala Prima/ Direct Approach

STUDIO PAINTING

COLORS: Burnt Umber, Raw Umber, Cadmium Red, Yellow Ochre, Cobalt Blue, Cerulean Blue, French Ultramarine Blue, Viridian Green, Ultramarine Violet, Prussian Blue

1   Best to paint the fine features of the eyes, nose and overall face first.

2   Next, let's paint the hat, mustache and beard second.

3   Finally, add in the background shapes loosely and casually, as it's a supporting feature in the composition. It is just some color and shape to keep the cowboy from looking too cut out and pasted down to the paper.

PHOTO.

Painting figures and portraits like these are a great way to start having fun with this subject matter. This was an antique black and white photo I saw online that had a sepia-tone look to it.

Red Winged Blackbird

This is a really fun painting to do!
I used a wood- painted carving as
my subject matter.

1 Start out contour drawing this blackbird.

2 Next, we will use our dark hues, such as
Paynes Gray, Ivory Black, Burnt Umber and
French Ultramarine Blue, to paint in the
colors on our blackbird. Once the Blackbird
is completely painted in, let it dry 100
percent.

3 Now we add in some background light
washes of the colors we used for the bird.

4 Add in some very sparse splashes over the
background washes and you have a great-
looking painting!

Shorebird Painting

Here, we will have a go at a lovely and charming shore bird! It is a simple composition that we can all create.

1   Start out with a light preliminary sketch and then go over top with a darker contour drawing, if you need to.

2   Next, we add in the darkest colors of this bird — including the back feathers, eye and beak — as well as the dowel that extends up from the base.

3   We now paint the background colors of Burnt Umber, Raw Umber and Cerulean Blue to create the look of the white tablecloth.

4   Add in the last few splashes and spattering of paint to finish up the painting.

Figures in Sunlight

In this painting we are going to push the boundaries of strong sunlight and solid shadows. Let us leave large amounts of white paper in this painting. Recall that you can add some light washes of warm and cool color to the white paper once you have completed the overall painting.

1 Start out with a good preliminary sketch and then subsequent contour drawing.

2 Paint in the figures first, along with the light washes of the sidewalk/ground areas.

3 Next, we can add the orange and reds of the clay-tile roofs. Take a break now and let everything dry.

4 Now we can add in the vibrant greens and golds of the trees at the furthest distance in the painting.

5 Last thing to do is splash in some very light washes to the stucco walls. Try to add a bit more warmth in the wash next to the seated figure; it will make that area seem to project closer to the foreground of the painting.

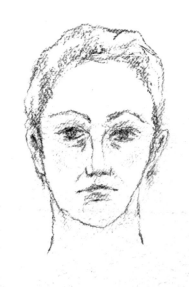

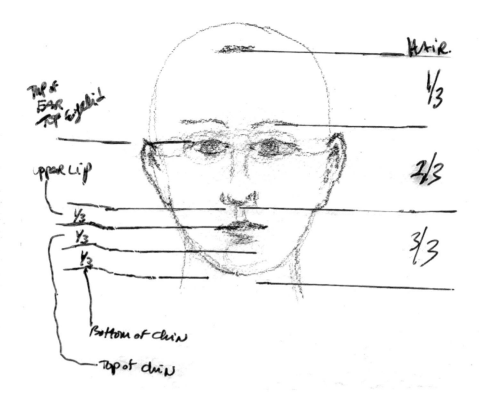

HAiR.

Top of
EAR
Top eyelid

1/3

upper lip

2/3

1/3

1/3

1/3

3/3

Bottom of chin

Top of chin

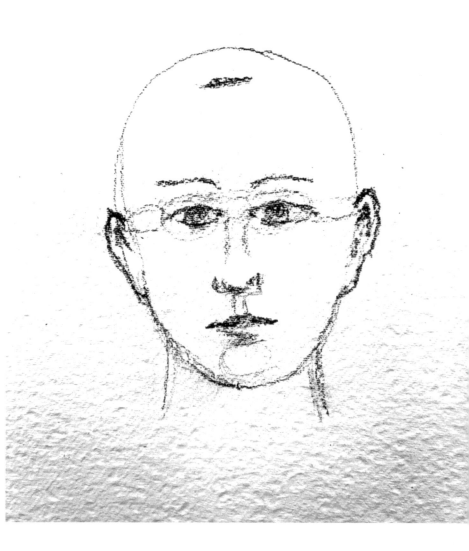

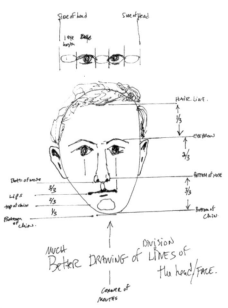

Side of head   Side of head

1 eye   eye
length   length

HAIR LINE.

1/3

EYEBROWS

2/3

Bottom of nose

Bottom of nose

3/3

Lips

3/3

top of chin

1/3

Bottom of
chin.

Bottom of
Chin

MUCH
BETTER DRAWING of LINES of DIVISION
the head/FACE.

corner of
mouth

6

ABOUT THE AUTHOR

Chris Petri

Chris Petri is an emerging Watercolor Artist from the United States. Predominantly a self-taught Artist, he has strived to continuously learn and study with the attitude of being a lifelong student of the Watercolor medium, logging in over 50,000 hours of study and viewing and studying over 100,000 watercolor paintings. His traditional style is perfect to study and emulate for newer students, as well as established artists. Chris tremendously enjoys the instructional aspects of his professional art career. He has been creating instructional videos on YouTube since 2016, with a fan base of tens of thousands of subscribers. Enjoy the exciting and vibrant colors, along with the loose and fun look that his paintings display.

Website: **ChrisPetri.com**

YouTube: **www.youtube.com/user/cpetri766**

Manufactured by Amazon.ca
Bolton, ON

33197976R00042